1000 Pieces of Time

1000 Pieces of Time © 2025 Michael Minassian

Cover photo: Michael Minassian
Author photo: Sue Minassian

ISBN: 978-1-962405-36-2
Library of Congress Control Number: 2025946351

Sheila-Na-Gig Editions
Russell, KY
Hayley Mitchell Haugen, Editor
www.sheilanagigblog.com

1000 Pieces of Time

Poems

Michael Minassian

Sheila-Na-Gig Editions

Advance Praise

In this impressive new collection, we immediately encounter Achilles, Marlowe, Amelia Earhart, Lot, Hamlet, Emily Dickinson, Dante, Cromwell, Helen of Troy, Darwin, Trotsky, the Buddha, et al. Clearly, Michael Minassian covers a lot of territory. His engaging blend of realism and surrealism adroitly develops his principal themes: desire, death, and—as his title reflects—the numerous changes wrought by the relentless passing of time. With its precise diction, creative imagery, and wise insinuations, this volume will enrich your poetry shelf.

—George J. Searles, editor/publisher of *Glimpse Poetry Magazine* and author of *Escape from Jersey City*.

Michael Minassian's distinctive voice propels his new collection, *1000 Pieces of Time*, into spirited engagement with memory, history, and the malleability of time itself. From encounters with Achilles on the subway, to Emily Dickinson at a restaurant (where we see "she was working as a waitress / at a Waffle House off I-95, / wearing a Boston Red Sox / baseball cap and / hot pink lipstick"), to Helen of Troy at Trader Joe's, we indulge ages past, present, and future with resonant rhythm. Blending observation and meditation, crafting with wit and sincerity, adding generous dashes of mortality and legacy, Minassian ferments this rich emotive brew by careful balance of precision and surrealism, serving up poems profound and immediate, poems that stick to the heart like bitter honey.

—Michael Dwayne Smith, author of *Shaking Music from the Angry Air*

This is a book of diversions and discoveries. It leaps through time shattering it to shards. We're in ancient Egypt, looking at the house next door, in a future with time machines. References reach from haute to pop, from today's news to classic films, famous writers, though none shows up as you'd expect. The book comes in three parts. The first features historic characters in today's world, Achilles on a subway, Kit Marlowe in a bar. Minassian's whimsies are funny but resonant, bon-bons with nutritious ingredients. Among the pleasures are Minassian's original tropes, metaphors to mull, similes to savor. In Part Two the poems turn dreamlike, enigmatic, anchored by the poet's sensibility. Part Three offers lyric adventures, what-if tales, serious family stories. This fine collection is unpredictable, unpretentious, addictively entertaining.

—Robert Wexelblatt, author of *Girl Asleep and Other Poems* and *Hsi-wei Tales*

Acknowledgments

The following poems have appeared (some in slightly different form) in the following periodicals, to whose editors grateful acknowledgment is made:

Artifactuals: "I Will Speak for the Bees," "To Turn Back Time"
Atticus Review: "Amelia Earhart on Long Island"
Baltimore Review: "Cathedral of Time"
Black Coffee Review: "Horatio Answers the Phone"
Cholla Needles: "Oliver Cromwell's Head," "Scenes From a Magazine," "Walking Backwards"
Eunoia Review: "Rehearsal"
Fourth & Sycamore: "Wild West Show"
Glimpse: "Dinosaur Dreams," "Lunar Blues," "The Poetry Conference"
Hye Bred: "Past Lives"
Live Encounters: "At the French Bakery," "Darwin's Beard," "Dressing the Buddha," "Film Noir," "Hieroglyphs," "It's a Black & White World, Again," "Memory," "Old Friends," "Silver Alert"
Lothlorien Poetry Review: "Desire"
Main Street Rag: "The Waitress"
Mojave River Review: "A Crow Can Fly in the Dark," "Between Design and Desire"
Muddy River Poetry Review: "How We Bury Our Dead," "November," "While I Slept"
Poetica: "Rose City"
Poetry Society of Texas: "Celluloid and Dust," "Hard Luck Line"
Rat's Ass Review: "Trotsky in Mexico"
Rise Up Review: "Tourist From the Future"
The Rye Whiskey Review: "The New Ice Age"
Sheila-Na-Gig online: "The Next Hurricane"
Slant: "Come Early, Leave Late," "The Sweet Spot," "The True Story of Lot,"
Somerville Times: "Lilacs Come Undone"
South Florida Poetry Journal: "Kemet"

The Arboriculturist (Chapbook): "Hills of Memory"
Third Wednesday: "Martha Stewart Invents My Kitchen"
Visions International: "Christopher Marlowe Buys Me a
     Drink," "Dante Reads a Book"

I would also like to thank the following editors, friends, and poets for their support and input: Michael Blanchard, Linda Goin, Beth Honeycutt, James Lewis, Liana Minassian, George Searles, Michael Dwayne Smith, Mark Ulyseas, and Robert Wexelblatt. As always, thanks to my wife Sue for her support.

Dedicated to all the teachers who showed me the way

"Time is the substance I am made of. Time is a river which sweeps me along, but I am the river; it is a tiger which destroys me, but I am the tiger; it is a fire which consumes me, but I am the fire."

—Jorge Luis Borges, *Labyrinths*

Contents

1.

2.

3.

1.

Achilles in the Underground

It's been a while
since I rode the subway

and I'm surprised to find
Achilles riding downtown

wearing a short tunic
and bright shining armor.

Like many riders, he's scowling,
but this is the underground,

and he may not be the only one
who's unhappy or dead.

When the lights flicker
and the train stops

between stations, I notice
the other passengers

shift nervously
as he lifts his sword

and gets to his feet,
but he's only giving up

his seat to an old
woman all in black

like the widows of Troy
dressed like crows

before they leapt
off the wall.

The Hills of Memory

They say the owl was a baker's daughter.
Lord! We know what we are,
but not what we may be.
                                —Ophelia

In the evening with the sun gone
I could see the stars appear
one by one, then in pairs,
trees deep dark green
stark against the disappearing gray,
silhouetted like the hills of memory.

There, near a row of pines
feet cushioned by the dewing grass,
I thought of the owl
that was the baker's daughter;
was she chaste as a bird,
the heat of hunger in her breast
chasing prey at night, the push
and rush of wings as currents
of wind stroked back feathers,
talons out, sweeping low to the ground,
striking and feeling the last frantic
beats of some creature's heart,
beak parted, eyes so wide
she could almost fly backwards
through her sight;
at that moment, did she remember
all the way back to her other life,
the smell of bread, the taste of sweet cake.

Christopher Marlowe Buys Me a Drink

At first, I don't recognize
the person sitting
on the next bar stool.

His hat pulled down low
over his forehead,
I hear him order an ale
in a clipped British accent,
& realize his clothing
has a distinct
16th century look.

Christopher Marlowe? I ask.

Call me Kit, he replies,
fingering his wispy moustache,
and winking at me
with his one good eye.

We talk for a while
about theatre, exotic birds,
and the British monarchy,
but he makes no mention
of Ben Jonson or Shakespeare.

When I get up to leave,
he offers to buy me a drink.
*These vagabond seasons
are out of balance,*
he complains,
and somehow, I know
just what he means,
our hearts full,
dense as time.

Amelia Earhart on Long Island

I once met Amelia Earhart
coming out of a general store
on the North Shore of Long Island
back in 1974.

I knew it was her because
of the leather aviator's cap
she wore pulled down on her head
and the antique brass sextant
she gripped in her hand.

She wanted to know
if I'd seen her navigator,
Fred, and asked me to drive
her down to the beach.

Walking along the sand,
she pointed to an object
sticking out of the water,
asking if it was her Lockheed plane,
but I tell her no, it's just a rock
the locals call Dead Man's Elbow.

Puzzled, I ask her about
the Japanese and Nikumaroro Island;
instead, she tells me the things
she misses the most:
cherry blossoms and snow,
and says the beach here
reminds her of Kitty Hawk.

When I was a child
I collected feathers
until I had enough
to make two small wings—
climbing up onto the roof.

I'd like to say I jumped off
and survived the fall,
but our neighbor saw me
and called my parents
who coaxed me down
with ice cream and a new
Felix the Cat clock.

Amelia cried when she saw the clock,
recognizing Felix from silent cartoons
she had seen in movie theaters
before she traveled around the world.

She understood flying happened
in the mind first, like sex,
or poems, words circling the globe,
some crashing in the ocean,
language a matter of timing
and good weather
rain and waves held in place
by the moon and tides.

I watched her leave my house—
the short walk down the driveway
and when she got to the sidewalk
she leaned down to scratch
the ear of my neighbor's dog,
the one with one eye,
who does not care about the past
and has no concept of the future tense.

I knew I would never see her again,
but looked up her name
in my copy of the Britannica,
finding a picture of Amelia
standing next to a sleek silver Electra—
this confluence of time and sand:
a single photograph
her unmarked grave.

The True Story of Lot

Drunken Angel
You're on the other side
—Lucinda Williams

He should have known
not to play with fire
or pray to a vengeful God—
never invite strange men
into his house,
let them eat his bread
and drink jugs of wine.

Forget about the wings
they pushed and preened
in front of his wife
and daughters.

In the city, word of Lot's
visitors spread—
a posse showed up
at the front door
and demanded to be let in.

Drunk and angry, the angels
blinded them with a brilliant
flash of light
then burned the city down.

When Lot's wife cried out,
they turned her
into a pillar of salt,
and left her on the road.

Later, Lot's daughters
claimed Moab and Ammon

were their father's sons,
but the hard nubs
on the boys' shoulders,
vestiges of wings,
told a different story.

Lot left to mourn alone,
as the stars shrugged
and his wife's shadow
trailed behind.

Horatio Answers the Phone

Next time send me a text,
everybody's calling,
wondering if those rumors
about my suicide are real:
I'm still here,
but yeah, Hamlet's gone,
stabbed in Central Park.

You remember we'd see him
in the Village dressed in black
hanging around Washington Square,
muttering about his dead father
and over-sexed mom.

His shrink kept asking
about his mother and uncle—
what did he feel,
how did she die,
who put the poison in her cup?

Wanted to know about his girlfriend too;
you remember she jumped in front
of the A train late one night—
claimed her father and brother
messed with her after her mother died.

But I gotta get back to NYU—
some professor named Yorick
is giving a workshop:
everybody gets to play
a corpse at least once.

My skull, he said, smells
just like a baseball
he found once down in the Bronx,

right after it connected
with his best friend's head.

Emily at the Waffle House

Split lives—never get well
                    —E.D. 1862 letter to a friend

I once checked into a hotel
in a strange city,
at first not noticing
the slim young woman
who stood behind me in line.

The next morning at breakfast,
we shared a table
and she told me her name
was Emily Dickinson
from Amherst, Massachusetts.

She wanted to know if her hair
pulled back in a tight bun
made her look too old,
complaining that she missed
the 19th century and her sister Lavinia.

Surprised she didn't want
to discuss poetry or publishing,
we talked about pop culture,
music, and the latest fashions.

The next time I saw her,
she was working as a waitress
at a Waffle House off I-95,
wearing a Boston Red Sox
baseball cap and
hot pink lipstick.

She brought my coffee,

sat down across the table,
and we spoke for a while,
trading stories, catching up
where we had left off.

There's no escaping life,
she sighed and I agreed,
admiring the tattooed
rose on her left wrist.

I wished her well—
glancing back from the door,
I watched her write furiously
on her waitress pad, scrawling poems
instead of someone's breakfast order,
or writing letters to the dead
she would post later
on bathroom walls,
while she dreamt
of long-lost relatives and lovers.

A few months later,
I got a postcard
with a photograph
of a Newfoundland puppy
on the front and a single sentence
in her precise scrawl
written on the back:
Have you found anything precious?

I mailed my own postcard
back to her new address:
Half of poetry is language,
the other half
the hollow part
of thought, I wrote.

Silver Alert

Staring at the telephone,
Cordelia takes a sip
of her morning coffee,
waiting until the kids
are fed and at school,
her husband on his way to work—
watching the video clip
of her plea for her father's
safe return: forgiveness
measured in algorithms,
post-truth expressions,
and You Tube hits.

After lunch she visits the police,
then staples flyers to sign boards
next to posters for pets
and runaway teenagers:
the lost and permanently missing—
searching in homeless shelters,
park benches and alleyways,
cardboard boxes and tents—
calling hospitals every other day
and the morgue once a week.

Her bickering sisters tell her
not to bother, complaining
about their husbands
and the lover that they shared.

Some days, she looks along
the banks of the river,
dragging fishing nets behind her,
consulting palm readers
and brain surgeons—

His memory emptied:
a delicate delirium,
her father said.

(Once, unable to answer
Cordelia found language
rusted on her tongue)

She thinks to herself:
too much time has passed—
wondering if she would
recognize him dressed in rags
or walking with his sightless
friends, wearing dark glasses
or tapping a white cane,
hiding from men of stone
or the proximity
of his daughters' last words.

Dante Reads a Book

Dante cleans the counter
with a wet rag,
wiping his hands on his apron,
pushing aside the chipped cup
and yesterday's newspaper.

On the other end of the counter
the new waitress
leans both elbows
in front of her boyfriend,
ignoring the other customers
signaling from the booth by the door—

Dante watches, saying nothing—
outside, rain beats on the window,
music drifts in through the open door
as other customers come in and the waitress
pushes back her hair and picks up a pen.

He remembers his parents
telling him he was named
for a baseball player from Florida,
discouraging him from playing sports,
going to church or falling in love.

After work, Dante takes a bus,
sitting behind a young woman
with short black hair
and a heart shaped face.

The next day he sees her again;
each time he gets on the bus
he leaves a note for her,
until one day she sits next to Dante,
handing him a worn copy

of *The Divine Comedy*
inscribed with her name.

Stopping at the East River,
Dante and Beatrice
abandon land for water,
boarding the ferry
circumnavigating the city—

vague shadows appear
as they pass under
the bridge at Hell Gate,
following a slow line of currents

riding all night
and through the next day,
seven circles, seven visions
chased by clouds

shaped like a long sleep,
and archaic memories,
turning time into words:

a lion's tooth
a tiger's wish
the throat of the wind

a second chance.

Elysian Fields

I.

In 1845, Albert Einstein
and Sir Isaac Newton
met at Elysian Fields
in Hoboken, New Jersey.

In clear view of the New York skyline
Einstein tested
his theories of relativity,
measuring the distance between
each of the bases and home plate.

When Newton came up to bat
he noted the speed of the ball
and the rate of descent,
as he tested his theory of gravity.

They challenged the New York Knickerbockers
to a seven-inning game
and played all the positions themselves.

II.

In Hiroshima, the bomb
that dropped from the Enola Gay
fell for the precise time
Newton had predicted.

On the school grounds that day
young boys played baseball
while hundreds of schoolgirls
cleared the fire lanes and watched
the ball fly, disappearing into the sun.
When the bomb exploded,

stitches on the baseball melted
exposing its inner core—
all the children burst into flames,
some sucked up into the mushroom cloud
despite gravity, mass, or matter.

The first time I saw photographs
of Hiroshima survivors,
their skin hung as limp
as the banners over home plate,
their eyes empty as zeroes
on the scoreboard.

I rode my bicycle in circles that day,
the baseball cards around the rims
rat-a-tat-tatting like machine guns
while I cursed the sun,
and prayed for Hammerin' Hank Aaron
to hit a baseball so hard
it would never return.

III.

When Einstein died ten years
after the war ended,
a scientist sliced his brain,
then distributed pieces to his friends.

Newton was buried under an ash tree:
two hundred years later
the tree was cut down
and made into baseball bats.

The Babe once tried the bat
and put it down—
feels hot, he said.

The Travel Agent's Poster

Last night, I walked along Main Street
past boarded-up store fronts
and abandoned shops,
and paused at the travel agent,
the one who closed for good.

In the window hung a poster
of Botticelli's Venus.

She was still on the clamshell
covering one breast
and her pubic bone
with strands of her hair.

I suppose the poster
meant to evoke Italy
and new beginnings.

But Venus looks pensive, even sad,
caught by surprise by the winds,
two blustery figures with wings
(never a good sign)
and a woman offering a cloak
covered with flowers
resembling spiders.

No wonder Venus looks down
and away, as if she knew
how beauty could be stolen,
how winter always crushes spring.

Oliver Cromwell's Head

The first time I encountered
Oliver Cromwell's head,
it was propped up on a dishwasher
in the back of a Korean restaurant.

The kitchen workers around me
either didn't see it or chose to ignore
the gruesome remains
of the Lord Protector.

Even when the head spoke,
complaining about papists
and the rights of kings,
they went on loading dirty dishes.

I wanted nothing to do with fanatics,
phantasmagoric apparitions,
politicians, or pretenders,
so backed out of the kitchen, too late.

The head floated like dandelion fuzz
just over my shoulder,
coming to rest on the center
of the dashboard of my car.

Better than a GPS, I thought to myself
as we drove off in search
of the closest Starbucks,
both of us in desperate need of caffeine.

When we passed a cemetery,
the head began to cry dry, hot tears—
skulls and fragments of bones
rose into the splintering air.

Grave diggers and mourners,
stopped in their tracks,
as the dead left their beds,
slack and unstuck with decaying flesh.

Above the freshly mown grass,
voices rose, everyone speaking at once—
random conversations,
this crossroad between life and death.

Cromwell's head floated into a cloud,
a final resting place at last,
I thought, but knew better—
his next life: no one left to protect.

Helen of Troy at Trader Joe's

Shoppers and staff
all turn to stare
as Helen of Troy

walks the aisles,
checking for organic products
and fills her basket

with golden fruit
and shapely produce
fit for a queen.

In the dairy department
she chooses Greek yogurt
and grass-fed milk,

then complains about
the lack of mirrors
and beauty products.

At the check-out
the cashier asks for
the secret to her perfect skin.

"Make sure a god
or at least a professional
baseball player

sleeps with your mother—
never eat eggs, keep away
from feathers and bird seed.

I'm allergic and hate
the sound I make
when I sneeze."

She pushes strands of hair
back over a shell-shaped ear,
a gift from Poseidon,

hums to herself,
hurries out to her car,
checking the sky

for odd-shaped clouds
passing arrows,
a disturbance of air.

Darwin's Beard

As a young man,
Darwin kept his beard
neatly trimmed, stray hairs
and fingernail clippings
preserved along with
insects and frog legs.

After returning
in the *HMS Beagle*,
he ran out of jars—
fossils and stuffed
birds kept in rooms
throughout the house,
ignoring the complaints
of his wife Emma
and the Anglican Church.

All the while his beard
grew whiter and longer—
when he slept at night
his beard stretched
to the next room
and out the door,
forcing his gardener
to mow lawn and beard
at the same time—
careful not to disturb
the nesting of gulls
or Emma's bone
and ivory combs.

In dreams he thought
he heard God cough
through His beard—
rimmed by dinosaurs,
doves, fossil wings
and angels braiding hair.

Rattling Locks

In portraits, Charles Dickens
looks straight ahead,
a wry smile on his face—
as the years pass,
he grows a beard,
poses only in profile.

Never tiring of happy endings,
compassionate in life and work,
he turns to rescuing orphans,
the crippled, and widows waiting
for their husbands lost at sea.

Even in old age he mourns
the death of his young sister-in-law,
visits her unused room
in his London home,
puts his ear to the floor
and hears a faint heartbeat,
wonders if he is dreaming.

Her dress remains on the bed;
he remembers the lisp when she spoke,
pictures the gap in her front teeth
grows as wide as the Thames,
teeth unfurl like sails
on a ship headed out to sea—

a muffled sound reaches his ear
as if the wind lost its voice—
he thinks he hears his name,
then a rustling like pages
turning by themselves.

Wild West Show

Buffalo Bill looked a lot
like Gen. Armstrong Custer,
especially when he wore
his fringed jacket
and thigh high boots.

Sometimes Sitting Bull
would chase Bill in the Wild
West Show, sighting him
down his rifle and smile.

(Not knowing he'd
be dead in 5 years,
shot by his own tribal
police, while Bill would die
in bed in another century).

Later, they walked arm
in arm from the main tent
along a muddy path
stained brown like a faded
sepia print, pausing once
in the rain as the ghost
of Crazy Horse galloped
overhead in a cloud,
the train whistle
blowing in the distance
as sharp as Custer's last cry.

A Crow Can Fly in the Dark

At the world's first rodeo
in Pecos, Texas,
lacking cash or prizes,
a young girl's dress
was cut into strips
and presented in place of prizes—
blue ribbons with tattered edges
like a bird's fallen wings.

The winners' names
recorded for all of history—
cowboys covered in glory,
but the girl's identity
never mentioned—
her nakedness forgotten.

(I wonder if her parents
and visiting farmers
and ranchers turned away,
protecting the modesty
of all mothers and daughters.)

Some say she hid among the crows
scavenging in the cattle pens—
covering herself with feathers and dung
before flying off the earth,
disappearing into the clouds and dust
as night's curtain fell
under a crescent moon.

Celluloid and Dust

John Wayne went crazy in *The Searchers*,
too much blood and heat—
his hair turned gray,
shooting out the eyes of the dead,
rocking in his brother's chair,
wearing buckskin and beads of sweat.

When the filming was over,
John Ford told him to go home,
but the Indians in Monument Valley invited
Wayne to a screening of their own movie:
teepees and thunderbirds racing through the desert,
skeletons and scalps hanging
from the backs of ponies and convertibles
chased by Natalie Wood's drowned ghost;
buckets of arrowheads for sale
along the side of the road—
sun dancers and screenwriters
bringing offerings in Spanish and code,
celluloid and dust, trading them for one eye,
a lung, ribs, and his stomach stuffed with lead.

Trotsky in Mexico

He wonders where the heat
comes from,
sitting in the garden
with his shirt off,
stroking his beard
and writing manifestoes
by candlelight.

Some days he meets Frida—
first removing her skirt
and elaborate underwear.

Drinking vodka together,
he writes down
lines of Russian poetry
she says she will include
in her paintings
(but never does).

When the man with the axe
arrives, he greets him warmly,
preparing soup and avocado
for lunch, then escapes
seconds before the blade falls,
missing him,
instead hitting Frida's
painting of wild birds
locked inside a cactus.

A few weeks later,
a Russian speaking tailor
named Lev Davidovich
arrives in the Bronx
and opens a shop
on the corner of Tremont

and Third Avenues—
later hiring a Mexican
seamstress who paints
murals on the side
of abandoned buildings
strewn with slogans
in Russian and Spanish.

At night, they sit and smoke
together on the fire escape
drinking vodka and cold
bottles of American beer—
the revolution pausing
between two world wars,
away from *Koba's* reach
and the pyramid's gaze.

Unwinding the Past

This afternoon, the sky turned
a deep shock of blue
like a swath of canvas

in a Renaissance painting
with gold clad angels
and women with braided hair.

Overhead, crows fly
in erratic circles
defying gravity and math

then disappear behind
a cloud shaped
like a mermaid's tail.

Across the street
a few kids kick
a misshapen soccer ball—

it lands at my feet
like the head of a saint
separated from its neck,

a kind of delirium
when the past opens
its mouth to speak.

Dressing the Buddha

Coming home from my neighbor's house
one snowy afternoon,
I recognized Shakyamuni Buddha,
wearing only a thin robe,
walking barefoot along the road.
Unlike the Zen masters,
I knew I couldn't kill him
even if it was an illusion—
instead, I took off my coat
and draped it over his shoulders,
then took him home
for a cup of tea and bowl of rice.

After eating, we watched TV,
counting breaths during the commercials
though he seemed not to like
any of the shows, keeping his eyes
closed the whole time
until I switched to cartoons,
and he smiled for the first time.

As he got up to leave,
I asked him what it was like
to walk everywhere on the earth
but he didn't answer—
never speaking a single word
even when I gave him
my favorite sweater, wool cap, and gloves
along with my wife's warmest boots
(surprised at how small he was and thin).

Just as he was going out the door,
my wife came home—
of course, she recognized him right away
and noticed he was wearing her boots—

have you been meditating again?
she asked me, shaking her head,
you can take me shoe shopping
as soon as I put these groceries away—
but before the Buddha could cross the road
she ran after him and gave him her saffron
colored scarf, wrapping it gently twice
around his bare neck: *thanks*, is all he said.

2.

What Words Can Say

A few years ago
my friend sold her house
and moved to
upper New York State.

She likes the solitude,
adopted a dog,
and took in a stray cat.

Twice a year she sends
me a long letter
describing her life.

I live in a cabin in the woods,
she writes, *at night the moon*
looks like a saucer of milk
reflected in the lake.

Each time, I write back to her,
I pick a word out
of the dictionary
and pull it like a loose thread.

Whole sentences spill out,
disappear in the rain
like floating leaves
at the end of the week.

The Rose City

In Petra, we walked along
a rocky path towards the rose
colored stone temple—
just outside the entrance
beggars sold ancient coins,
swords, and bits of pottery
rubbed and weathered to look old.

The woman I loved smiled
for the first time that day
our last together—
like the god *Dushara*
and his consort
we faded into the shadows
of rock and sand.

Poets may speak of loss
and regret but the next
day brought only
knives of zero
and the dawn's empty hand.

Past Lives

I have often seen signs
of my past lives:
a stranger on the sidewalk,
a half-familiar face or gesture,
the shape and shadow of clouds,
or the swirl of snow
as the wind picks up,
and a solitary leaf spirals down
from the branch of a tree.

I dream of fabulous hotels
in Paris along the Seine,
dark barbarian hovels,
Roman legions, ancient cathedrals
in the shadow of Mount Ararat,
and treks with lamas in the Himalayas.

I watch a delicate dance of skeletons
exchange a crown of thorns
in a long unbroken line of famine,
powdered wigs, and gleaming guillotines.

I know a multitude of mantras
and prayers in many languages—
are these the threads
of reincarnated lives?

Perhaps it is all an endless loop,
repeating the same events
across dimensions and strings
of time held tight and plucked
like an instrument tuned to a key
heard just beyond the horizon.

Hieroglyphs

A woman I knew
was afraid of rain,
stains that would not wash away.

She ate tomatoes like apples,
biting into the flame red flesh,
soft as sex, wet as lashes.

She told me once love
felt like being buried alive,
as if it was the last squeeze
of the Pharaoh's kiss.

I painted hieroglyphs
of boats sailing down a river—
the vague utterances
of fish and ibis
followed every move.

We spoke in a dead language,
chanting incantations
only the two of us understood—

too late, the boatman
waited on the far shore.

Kemet

When I wake up in the morning,
I'm covered in gold foil;
convinced I'm in ancient Egypt—

Outside my window, a naked man
with the head of a white ibis
is mowing the lawn.

While I watch, he removes
each of his eyes, rinses them
with the garden hose,
then puts them back in their socket.

Later, I drive to the beach—
Ft. Lauderdale looks
like the Pharaoh's nightmare—
in place of bikini bars
there's an unfinished pyramid
and mummies stacked
up on the sand.

The palm trees look the same,
except for the archers
hiding in the fronds—
arrows whizz by my head—

A woman joins me—
she looks vaguely familiar,
and tells me we've been here before—
clouds cluster above us
like backward spinning clocks.

We hold hands—
our watches, hot, like fresh
baked bread, the smell of time
on our wrists.

Tourist From the Future

When the first tourist from the future
appeared, he took photographs
with a tiny camera the size
of a baby's tooth, all the while
complaining about the bright
sunshine & lack of public toilets.

The are no birds in our world,
& fish no longer have bones,
he told the television reporter
on Channel 4, *but,* he boasted,
we have condos on the moon,
& one government on Earth.

When pressed, he could not
say whether his visit
was prompted by science
or tourism, but professed
an overwhelming nostalgia
for the past, though he no longer
cared about history, pop culture,
or current events.

Don't worry about
what is to come, he shouted
as he climbed into his time machine,
the past goes whizzing past
your head like a bullet.

The rest is all made up.

Walking Backwards

I.

Born in Savannah,
they called her Mary
a name she abandoned later;
her mother shielding
her from the poor
who crowded tenements,
& back streets,
as her father wasted
away from lupus.

II.

When Mary was five years old
she practiced teaching
animals to dress & talk.

Though they could not speak,
she trained one,
small black rooster,
to walk backwards—
the youngest star of tabloids
and Pathé movie newsreels:
Little Mary & Her Chicken.

Sometimes her mother let her
play with a little girl next door
extolling them to be quiet.
They would tiptoe
down the hall
into the bathroom.
Mary sat on the toilet seat
reading Grimm's fairy tales,
her friend listened,
sitting in the empty tub.

III.

She learned to name
the creatures, wolves, & witches
that tore through her dreams,
chopping, hacking, & stealing
eyelids and grandmother's
wooden leg in the name of God,
& an inverted childhood
where parents disappeared
into forests, ovens, & coffins.

V.

Later, she took the name Flannery,
writing her own life
in another Georgia town
sick from her father's inheritance,
returning to her mother's home
in a hospital train.

The house materializing
like a broken bathtub
from the ambulance bed—
too sick to move on her own.

VI.

Her room part infirmary
part writing studio;
her stories peopled w/ friends
& neighbors, mothers, & monsters,

Grim tales for the new world,
she emptied herself
of memory & desire
until nothing remained

but books & the braces
she used to walk backwards
into one last dark Georgia forest.

To Turn Back Time

Who goes there? What's the password?
— Ray Bradbury

I'm standing in the kitchen
boiling a watch,
trying to turn back time.

I have a certain nostalgia
for both the past,
and the promise of a future
with flying cars, moving sidewalks,
robotic homes, and chic unisex
clothing made of silver thread—

My friends complain
about the lack of a cure;
their faces shine with sweat
as they remove their masks,
offering me a few drops
of disinfectant or a glass of wine.

I've lost my sense
of taste and smell,
pass by empty
supermarket shelves,
and vaccination camps.

Outside, refrigerated trucks
hold the dead
like heads of wilted lettuce;
water drips into pools
on the pavement below.

The Mayans buried their dead
inside the home,

smashing through walls
and digging up the floors.

I've knocked down the fence
between my house
and the neighbor's garden;
their voices silent,
the world as quiet
as a spider's next move.

The Cathedral of Time

When my uncle died,
my aunt smashed
all the clocks in the house,
unplugged the TV
and her telephone,
hung mirrors on every wall.

In case he comes back,
she whispered,
I want to see him first.

When I offered to drive
her to the cathedral,
she handed me the keys:
keep your foot on the gas,
she cried, *I don't want to be late.*

At the service,
the priest talked
about resurrection,
and families re-uniting—
a brief window into eternity.

I walked away
scattering broken
pieces of clocks,
like rice at a wedding
of time and death.

How We Bury Our Dead

In ancient Jordan,
children who died were placed
in clay jars and stored
under the floor of the home
to keep them
in the family circle.

In Egypt, mummies were buried
with a golden tongue nestled
in the jaw bone:
the tongue made of gold foil
meant to help the deceased
converse with Osiris
on their way to the afterlife.

In the computer age,
the dead keep their profiles:
emails, texts, and messages—
while we wait for someone else
to hit the delete key,
not knowing how to mourn
while anniversaries and birthdays
return as reminders when all
other symbols are gone.

November

The crows on the fence
in the backyard
solemn as Druids,
nod to each other
& call out
crazed incantations.

The sky as blue
as a glacier's heart—
cold wind cracks branches,
leaves fall from trees,
& whip across the yard.

Better to hunker down,
lock all the doors
thumb through old books,
& watch the slowly
sinking sun.

Stay away, you want to cry—
the world outside
unfurls like an angry lover,
who, too late, realizes
the affair is over,
& pours poison in your ear
while you sleep.

The Next Hurricane

Preparing for a Cat 3 storm,
I help my neighbor
board up his windows;
he asks me later
if I was Italian or Jewish,
but when I tell him no,
Armenian, he nods as if
it was another piece of bad news.

Overhead, a flock of geese
fly in a tight V formation
dropping brown and white
turds on the roofs
across the street,
see what I mean? he asks,
It's going to be a shitstorm.

But that was ten years ago,
he and his wife long gone,
their house repossessed;
another family live there now,
hurricane-shy,
leaving their shutters up
all year long.

I fall asleep with the radio on,
dream of a chiseled distance,
sift for clues in the sand;
somewhere cartographers
draw new boundaries,
storms gather off shore—
the weather reported
in a series of metaphors:
spaghetti paths,
cone of uncertainty,
the mother of all storms.

I'll call the next one Medusa,
wait for winter, turn to stone.

Almost Holy

The day after Christmas
we drove to the beach
and pushed the butt end
of the umbrella
deep into the sand;
I found no signs of snow
or ice or decorations
other than the whirl
of foam as the surf
broke on the shore.

If this wave was born
of Bethlehem
over two thousand years ago,
it happened out of sight
of priests or parents or potentates,
perhaps a shifting of sand
out in the desert,
or a tremble along
some broken mountain chain,

as unlikely as the solitary
crab who emerges
from its hole
and skitters
across hot sands
towards the cool blue
of the Atlantic
under the gathering
scarab of clouds.

Up on Cemetery Hill Road

The Jehovah's Witness
Kingdom Hall

is next door
to the Lutheran Church

the parking lots separated
by a stone wall

the congregants
play softball against each other

Sunday afternoons
waiting for the umpire

to call out their names
as they cross home plate

each base like a station
of the cross

understanding the metaphors
of summer afternoons:

curve ball, hit or miss,
squeeze play, sacrifice fly.

Heaven a long way—
an even longer walk

than over the stone
wall next door.

While I Slept

It stormed last night;
I heard the wind
drive the rain
against the windows,
a noise like horses' hooves
rattling across a wooden bridge.

In the morning,
a parade of black birds
crossed my lawn,
the grass wet,
their feathers shining
like armor as if
they were ready
to take back the world.

History an invisible tattoo
itching under the skin,
lurking while we sleep.

Rehearsal

I.

Those hills in the distance
turn a rose color,
like a hummingbird's tongue
stretched to taste the dawn.

Behind the hills,
the shadow of ancient cities
moves across the face of the sun
like random words.

On a low wall surrounding
a library of forgotten dreams
a lone figure sews together a clock.

II.

Like a luminous thought
or an encyclopedia
of exacting numbers,
a mist surrounds you—
a scrambled alphabet
woven over time.

Notes fragile and bright,
a heartbeat from another century,
a string plucked, then another.

III.

Foggy with dreams,
you regret the space between sleep
and the broken thread you followed
out of the labyrinth of lucid reflections.
Time flickers,

light always out of reach
clocks stitched from soft patches:
clouds tipped on their sides.

You've left behind the study of geography,
created your own maps—
a cartography of caverns and catacombs
even upon the calligraphy
you drew on the city.

Overhead, skyscrapers and cathedrals,
spires, the cult of coins, and spoils of war
compete for a lottery of languages
not yet invented, forgotten
for a thousand years.

Inside the room,
the dialogue holds a logic
only you can understand.

Old Friends

Last night our friends
came by for dinner—
we hadn't seen each other
for over ten years.

We cooked a feast,
filled counters and table
with grapes and cheese,
fruit pies and chocolate cake,
bread, tureens of soup,
rice, potatoes, vegetables,
bottles of wine and cold drinks.

All of us so full,
we could barely push ourselves
away from the table,
telling stories of the past—
family histories and legends
about growing up in the Bronx,
under the shadow of the 3rd Avenue El,
not far from the cottage where Poe
lived with his mother-in-law
and wife (and first cousin) Virginia
who coughed up blood
while playing the piano,
then died a few years later.

Poe stayed up nights,
language stalled,
while he waited for the dead
to rise like yeast,
stuck in limbo or disbelief,
cursing his fate:
all the women he loved
dying from TB.

Hoping his next life will be better,
free from disease and memories
of loss, premature burials,
and the pendulum's breath—
a life with refrigerators
and iced tea, music,
poetry, and old friends
on the back porch.

Compassion

I say, drop a mouse into a poem
                              —Billy Collins

When I dropped a mouse into my poem,
he seemed lost at first,
wandering between images,
chewing on the ends of lines,
swallowing whole metaphors,
and leaving dark, hard droppings
like random punctuation.

Later, other mice
frightened and hungry,
stumbled into the poem,
like Greek wanderers
sacrificed to the Minotaur—
a labyrinth of broken lines
and missing links,
until the first mouse showed the rest
which words were safe
to eat and which held hidden
dangers or poison puns,
navigating between stanzas
and empty spaces
leading towards the edge
of the white page,
sailing to the end of the world.

You Get Three Wishes

It's no use thinking
the genie that just popped
out of the lamp

you found at the garage sale
will grant you
another wish.

The old woman
with the snaggle tooth
warned you, "Don't bring

it back here, sonny."
But you thought it
was a real bargain

coming like it did
with three wishes
and its own Immortal.

Too bad when you asked
for an extra wish,
it was against the rules.

Now you've traded places
with the ex-genie curled up
on the couch with his hand

up your wife's t-shirt,
the other hand
holding the remote,

and you wonder
if the next time
someone rubs that lamp

will he want a second
chance, a new kidney,
two pink lungs,

or to turn back time,
escape from inside
that hunk of tarnished brass.

Memory

In the back of the closet
I find a roll of undeveloped
black and white film.

As I hold it in my hand,
I try to remember where
or when I had taken the photos

and why they had never
been developed;
a mystery making me shiver.

Some things are better
left undisturbed—
a locked door at the end of the hall,

a letter from a former friend,
the final steps to the basement
as the light goes out,

memory's blast of winter,
and a spider's voice
only you can hear.

Hard Luck Line

The last day of January
breaks like a dry twig—

cold wind,
blue sky.

The dirt in the garden
hard as a villain's heart.

Along the railroad tracks,
gray cinders,

weeds thick as rope—
a small white cross

all that's left
of someone's bad luck.

The Sweater

Today, I notice
a thread unraveling
on the sleeve of a shirt.

I think of my grandmother
and her sewing box
crammed with needles and thread.

A proud, lifelong member
of the International Lady
Garment Workers Union

she kept her membership
card with her citizenship
papers and the photo

of my grandfather
in his handsewn shirt
next to her bed.

Yet I knew she worked
in harsh conditions
at a time when clothing

was made in the USA,
and immigrant women
worked long hours

in poorly lit factories
with no ventilation.
America had its own

sweatshops, children
worked in warehouses
instead of going to school.

A survivor of the Genocide,
she walked through the desert
from Armenia to Lebanon

before coming to America.
At her funeral, I sat
holding her favorite sweater,

a worn wool cardigan
I brought home
from the hospital,

the top two buttons
missing, as absent
as her voice.

Follow the Light

My cousin John
older by five years,
taught me to play basketball,
how to eat a taco.

When he died,
I kept waiting for him
to come back from the dead.

After all, his brother,
my other cousin, was a priest,
and Jesus raised Lazarus
from the grave after 3 days.

I remember other stories
of people clinically dead,
revived somehow,
who spoke of a light
they followed like traffic signs
in the Lincoln Tunnel,
coming out again, alive,
on the other side.

Instead of grief, I feel anger,
and wonder what my aunt
would say, her whole family
in Armenia killed in 1915,
ghosts haunting
her house on Long Island,
already crowded,
jostling for space with John.

The Poetry Conference

Every labyrinth has its minotaur
—Carlos Ruiz Zafón

I arrive early at the poetry conference,
see a few familiar faces,
stop to say hello
and renew old acquaintances.

Near the back of the room;
seats around me fill up quickly—
the workshop leader prompts
us each to write a poem.

I squint my eyes,
sneak a look at other poets,
heads down or staring into space,
a few pulling out their hair.

At one table a bull sits alone,
his black coat slick with sweat;
I imagine steam escaping
from each of his nostrils,

try to start a conversation,
but he ignores me,
snorting once and pawing
at the table with his rough hooves.

The room darkens as if a rain cloud
joined us in a mythic moment
of delusion, a maze of words,
images brushed aside or abandoned.

Nothing rhymes, he bellows—
soon it's lunchtime

and the other poets flee,
leaving me alone with the bull,

who stomps out without a word
or glance in my direction,
a thin sheaf of papers
fluttering in his angry wake.

When the next session begins,
I read my poem,
wave metaphors like a red cape,
like handwriting in the sand.

3.

Scenes From a Magazine

The pine tree outside my window tries to speak. Pine needles wag like sharp little green tongues. Are they words of warning in tree speak? When the wind calms, there is a hush like black rocks ringing the pond. The wind picks up again. The branches nod yes, they nod no. Tongue, bark, lips, needles, foot, a network of fungal mycelium, tiny threads that wrap around or bore into roots. I can't hear them or know what they say. They hear me, I speak again. Then there is quiet.

The residents of the mental hospital spill down the road, clamoring for drugs, alcohol, cotton to stuff their ears. Nurses, doctors, orderlies run after them. They all return to the hospital. For twenty years, they say, spirits roam the halls at night. Keeping the lights on 24 hours a day doesn't help. From down the hill, the building looks like an open skull with moonbeams inside.

The old woman in the house next door shows me her collection of old postcards. One has a photo of the body of a killer whale washed up on a beach. I'm surprised to see I sent it to her the year before I was born. The address is the same, the driveway in need of paving, the curtains torn.

I found a letter an old girlfriend had sent to me a few years ago. At the time, I didn't bother reading it. This time I sat down and proofread it carefully, correcting the grammar and punctuation. It seemed she was willing to forgive me and give me a second chance. I didn't believe a word of it. When I was through with my corrections, cross outs, and erasures I could barely make out the word goodbye carved into my skin.

The Waitress

Even before I sat down
the waitress brought
a cup of coffee to my table—

striking up a conversation,
we talked about
our favorite movies,

the fragrant leaves of summer,
the shape and texture of skin,
and the exotic taste of mangoes.

Through the plate glass
window we could see
a shelf of sunlight

rearranging itself
along the horizon
in an intimate gesture,

reminding us of other
stories we might tell
outside this place

our bodies leaning towards
each other like metaphors
from undiscovered poems.

Desire

That green and white
hummingbird
who appeared outside
the French doors
hovered and darted
around the purple
Phalaenopsis orchid.

Desire looks like this—
the brightest bloom,
the tug of air,
an eye in motion,
when everything
else is still.

Martha Stewart Invents My Kitchen

She's all business
as she steps through the door,
cleaning the counters
of forgotten appliances,
empty cereal boxes
and take out cartons.

She washes the dishes,
empties the fridge,
and sweeps the floor
until the kitchen
is as tidy as a jail cell.

When I ask her
when I can start cooking,
she smiles and says, *never*,
like a blind date
that went on too long.

All day and half the night,
she chops vegetables,
grates cheese, whips cream,
and kneads bread,
filling dish after dish,
readying a banquet
for a dozen guests or more.

When she finishes,
I help her carry
everything out to her car,
What now? I ask,
sneaking a cookie
while her back is turned.

You're on your own,
she says, *but keep*
that kitchen clean
or I'll be back.

Typical Jersey girl,
I think, glad to see her go
and have the kitchen to myself,
the happy chef of catastrophe.

Le Bureau Des Taxis

The small office
under the railroad bridge
is gone, along with the bar
up the hill.

That's the last place
I saw one of the drivers
as he left the bar,
stumbling and weaving
down the road,
his girl friend
chasing him
in her bare feet,
the two of them
looking like fish
thrown up on land
mouths opening
and closing
with every step.

I'd swear I saw gills
on both their necks
leaking foam
and star fish—
a string of curses
spilling on the road
like shards of sea glass
after the tide goes out.

I wish I could have frozen time,
caught them in mid-stride,
given them a whole new
set of speeches, dialogue
from some New Wave film,
painting words on the pavement

like sub-titles to replace
the fish-hook memories,
the kind that stab you
in your eye while you're asleep.

At the French Bakery

The croissants line up
like the errant heads
of the aristocracy.

Napoleons march off
to the Russian Tea Room
or the island of desserts.

Baristas operate guillotines
cutting off the foam
of lattes and the sound

of the ocean, a mosaic
of musical notes:
la mer, la mer, la mer.

Behind the scenes
bakers line up beating
and kneading dough.

Mona Lisa moaning
in the bathroom stall
smiling to herself.

Baudelaire cutting
holes in his story
following Poe

waking to find
women rising like yeast
in a graveyard of bread.

Still hungry, you wander
into the kitchen
watching Madame Bovary

molding madeleines
into the petite shape
of a vulva:

the waiting room
of Proust's dreams
and the palate's abyss.

Film Noir

In a black & white world
tendrils of fog rise
from city streets, manhole
covers, and factories
that burn day & night.

All the men wear hats,
& women smoke
you with their eyes,
leading you down a trap
only a bullet can cure.

Children are urchins
or angels, depending
on the curl of hair
or cut of their clothes.

Mothers in aprons
wait at home,
wring their hands
as the clock ticks,
& the sun goes down,
throwing a lattice work
of shadow on shadow
across the room.

Somewhere in the dark
a whistling sound
approaches through the mist,
the single glow of a cigarette
pierces the screen
& light pours out,
colorless, bright,
& filled with stars.

Ahead only bad choices—
you can't see what's coming,
even though you've heard
this story before.

Fog, One Dreamy Night

They say fog obscures sight,
visibility zero or less.

The night I drove
to your house along the coast,

even the sudden appearance
of a riderless white horse

on the road, like something
out of a Luis Buñuel film,

its muffled hoof sounds
matching my heart beats,

couldn't mask the picture
of you in my mind—

waiting by the window
letting the fog waft in

to surround you,
white as your skin

the earth's steamy breath,
the weather of your cinema.

Baby, You're So Cruel

We travel down the highway,
riding as if we're stuck in some
mid- 20th century country music song,
all twangy guitar & fiddle
playing on the car stereo
with one busted speaker;
a persistent hum coming
from the passenger side—
I'm not sure if it's the radio
or you speechless with anger.

I ask you to check the map
one last time, but you say *no*,
the place we are going
isn't on any map,
and I should have known better
or at least stopped to ask directions
at the last town; *yes*, the one
with boarded up storefronts
and a post office with no zip code.

When we get to another fork
in the road, the signs point
in every direction, like fingers
on an abandoned scarecrow,
and the next time I look over,
you are gone, that hum I hear
nothing more than the wind
whistling through the top
of the window I left open a crack,
hoping you might still
slip back into the car.

Islands and Continents

When I had my first apartment,
there was an old water stain
on the ceiling
that looked like a map
of Antarctica.

The women I brought there
liked to stare at that spot
before we took off our clothes
and jumped into bed.

Sometimes my neighbor
banged on the wall
when we got too loud.

Later, I moved the bed
to the other outer wall
right under the window.

It was warmer there in summer,
and the map changed shape,
new continents and islands emerged.

Each time I brought someone home,
our nakedness rose to the ceiling—
we roamed far deserts and oceans.

My neighbor cried
when we pushed off from shore

away on the other side of the room.

The New Ice Age

My friend's wife called
to ask if she could stay
at our house but begged
my wife not to tell
my friend she was there.

When he called, I lied to him;
later, they got back together—
we never saw either one again.

Sixty-five million years ago
when an asteroid hit the earth,
dinosaurs became extinct
and the last ice age began—
the way I watched
my friend and his wife leave
my house, their footprints
filling up with snow,
birds circling overhead
in a slow spiral until
they were out of sight.

Dinosaur Dreams

—for Liana, at ten

Surrounded by books one night,
you cried after finding a small
patch of dried skin on your leg,
afraid you would soon be covered
in scales and feathers, reptilian remnants
of the great dinosaurs that fascinated you:
t-rex, triceratops, raptors, and your favorite,
the leather-skinned pterodactyls,
their long thin beaks like spears set
to pierce the armor of long lizards of fear—
in my imagination I stood guard alone
brandishing fire: dragon slayer, father,
keeper of dreams, protector, shaman, poet.

Lunar Blues

Tonight, lunar winds blow
although the air is still.

Moonlight covers us
like a fleeting thought.

How many times
have we looked up

at the moon,
how many times

have we said
we are sorry,

how many times
have we turned away?

Lilacs Come Undone

The dream is a slow waterfall—
birds fly through the mist;
they wear casual suits
made from feathers and bones.

Rain falls and shimmers
in the sunlight
like a school of fish
turning together in the sea.

Inside a burning house
bees play violins—
I eat chocolate cake
at the kitchen table.

My friend knocks on the front door,
bringing a bouquet of weeping women,
drowsy with sleep and grief,
like lilacs come undone.

I wipe away words
floating in the air,
the library of my mind
holds only a snapshot of verse.

Frozen in Time

Last night I spoke to an old friend
three thousand miles away

across three time zones,
catching up on missing years

lamenting those long gone,
our circle of writers and rivals

trading poems and lovers,
cold nights and hot dawns,

moments frozen in time
thawed by fading memories

like old haunts boarded up,
other names scrawled on blank walls.

Bruised Flowers

Sleep's wings
nest behind the eyes,
wait until dark
for the lingering scent,
blossoms and buds,
a pastry of trembling
in the evening mist.

Ancient Egyptians
believed the tears
of the sun god Ra
fell to the earth
and became honey bees.

The hummingbird
outside my window
appears to hover
in front of the orchid
its four chambered heart
beating twelve hundred
times a minute.

A dance of flight
to rival the bees,
numb the tongue,
colors of courtship,
wounded petals and rain.

The bee's dance
quickens and blurs,
circles back, signals
direction, richness
of pollen and scent,
returns to the temple
of bruised flowers,
nights of nectar,
to seduce the queen.

My Sister Dated Frankenstein

For a few months
my sister dated
Frankenstein's monster.

Stitch by stitch,
he made his mark
on our small town.

In high school, he played
football and basketball,
but was banned

for being too big
and breaking other
players' bones.

The movie theater
and bowling alley
both shut down

vowing to never
let him or other
creatures return.

He spent long hours
in the library devouring
books on history and culture,

read *Paradise Lost*
and taught himself German,
but claimed not to know

about the disappearance
of children and small pets,
or the drowning death

of my best friend
after he asked my sister
to the senior prom.

On dates, Frankenstein
took her to the cemetery
in the middle of town,

an ancient graveyard
dating back before
the Revolutionary War.

When she asked him,
what's it like to come
back from the dead

he said he couldn't
remember that many
lives: *I'm all in pieces.*

When she broke up with him,
his tears filled our backyard;
his heart shattered again.

The Sweet Spot (1962-1972)

The boy on the front porch
stares into the palm
of the baseball glove.

Baseball a game of statistics,
history, and metaphor:
at school he learns
the Greeks invented nepotism,
the Olympics, and the phalanx:
a rectangular battle formation
turned on its side,
diamond shaped
like a baseball infield.

Ten years later he stops for coffee
on his way back from the draft board,
washing his hands until the skin
peels off like a napalm kiss.

In Saigon, he wanders
from café-to-café missing home
and writing letters:
who won the World Series?
he wants to know,
who will win the war?

Was it really better
to be red than dead?

Remembering how it felt that day:
feeling summer coming on,
trying hard to compare
the heat in Vietnam
to the sound of the bat
as it hits the ball:
the sweet spot, they say,
hoping it's enough to stay alive.

Come Early, Leave Late

Like a bird confused by a warm winter day,
I arrive early at the funeral service.

The body in the open casket bears
a passing resemblance to the face

I saw in the mirror this morning,
except for its blue lips and pensive look.

The room is empty except for a few
folding chairs stacked up against one wall,

a vase of wilted lilies, and a guest book
with blank pages on a table with three legs.

If this was a dream, at this point
I might wake up, shake my head, laugh

at the absurdity, and grab a cup of coffee,
but when I pinch myself, it hurts.

The sound of voices and noise of caterers
setting up reaches me from the next room.

I know I'm too early, out of sync with time,
then reach into my pocket, pull out

my Swiss Army knife with the tiny scissors
and clip a lock of the corpse's hair.

Outside, a storm has gathered, angry
and gray. It's snowing, Winter again.

I hail a cab, and quiet as falling
light, I am gone, perhaps too late.

The View From the Bungalow,

—Sound Beach, Long Island

Down the hill
a huge stone
dropped by giants
on their way home.

In the garden
an apple tree
arms spread like winter
to catch the night's fall.

A low brick wall
to keep the neighbor's close,
the scent of warm bread
to awaken the past.

In summer, the rain
fills hollows on the road,
the sky reaches down
like a spoon.

Near the basement
steps, a rake, a tin pail,
a chipped ceramic mug
left on the outdoor sink.

A freshly mown lawn,
a red pump handle,
the way you remember—
scenes from a passing breeze.

Karpet

Dark blue, like the sky with the moon
the only light, other colors muted,

woven together into ancient ruins:
broken pottery, a touch of orchids,

the lotus flower in the center;
other branches, other blossoms

form the border, earth meets
mountains, some climb over each other,

some wander edge to edge
then fall off; clouds the color of earth,

earth the color of the dark blue sky,
the gates of the garden, broken to let us in.

I Will Speak for the Bees

The biography of the bee
is written in honey
                    —Linda Pastan

I rode in an elevator
from street level to penthouse,
a honeycombed hive—
sweetness like a bitter potion,
the worker's devotion,
the queen's empty grace.

She wears red slippers
embroidered with dragons,
reclines on a couch
covered with flower petals;
her wings vibrate the air
with the scent of pollen
and a humming noise
designed to drive
the drones mad with lust
as they sign up to mate
with her in flight, then die.

The heart knows
what it wants
but not who it wants—
I will speak for the bees,
the sting of love
fierce on my tongue.

The Widow Next Door

The widow's house
was piled high with
old postcards, love letters
and prayers she wrote
on napkins, post-it
notes, strips of wallpaper
she tore from the walls.

Some reminders,
to-do lists, groceries,
and household chores
(clean the garage,
wash the floor,
empty the trash),
pleas to God,
angels, and priests
for luck, love,
mercy and grace.

When the house
was full, she papered
the lawn, the oak tree
in her back yard,
her driveway, garage,
and the sidewalk that led
down the block.

I wonder if she peers
through the window blinds
and sees me when I read
each message as if
it had floated in a bottle
and found me shipwrecked
on this shore, marooned
with paper, pen,
and half-eaten words.

Barely Heard

Some poets have animals
populate their poems:
black birds, elephants, or mice.

They worry about crushing weight,
the scrabble of claws on the roof,
hear scratching behind the wall.

Their angels wear black wings,
follow each other tail by tail,
leave droppings under the sink.

Some poems poise on the pen
like a bird before it takes flight;
some lie in wait for words

to nudge themselves, stand
on two legs instead of four,
a rustle of fanning feathers,

the turn of a murder of crows,
the swish of a tail,
the sigh of breath, barely heard.

Even in Silence

There's a quiet noise
inside silence,
an architecture of sound.

The trees in the woods
nod their leafy branches
as if every word I speak

is in a language
we both can understand—
that and the wind.

Sometimes in a knot of wood
you can see a face,
a mouth about to flutter

like eyelashes on a fawn—
a moth's wings on fire
light fading, then gone.

Between Design and Desire

I am writing this simultaneously
in English & another language
which cannot be read
by anyone now living.

I have disguised
these words & lines,
or overlaid them; the dead
language resting comfortably
both under & on top of the living,
intertwined like lovers
from different centuries.

As you are reading this,
at least one other language
has become extinct
at a faster rate than birds,
mammals, fish, or plants.

What is gone between
an abacus & an Aztec
or even between
toast & a toothbrush?

How many words are there
for snow or rain or love or skin?

Covering a dictionary
with my tongue
I discover ten words
between design & desire
moments before they disappear.

It's a Black and White World, Again

In *Casablanca*, the Nazis have loud voices
and throw people out of windows,
or maybe they're just checking for rain—
everyone runs around going to secret meetings
or gambles at Rick's Place (and loses)
although the wheel is sometimes rigged.

Young women, married and single,
throw themselves at Rick who's
pretending to be Humphrey Bogart.

Claude Rains, who used to be *The Invisible Man*,
is Louie, a cop, and Rick's friend;
the people who work for Rick are all Antifa
disguised as waiters and Casino workers;
some of them speak in bad accents
and sing *La Marseillaise* while crying
and playing the guitar, except for Sam
who knows he better stay put.

In 1942, the Germans were Nazis
and they want to close Rick's place;
Rick's ex who dumped him in Paris
comes to his *Café Américain* gin joint
with her husband, a big Antifa,
who speaks with an Eastern European
accent and might be KGB or FSS.

Like many in transit in Casablanca
they covet transport papers
(as if a green card was a green light)
so they can fly to Portugal
then get to America on an airplane
even though Rick says:
They're all asleep in New York.

Oh, and Sidney Greenstreet wants to stay
in Casablanca, since he's a capitalist
and doesn't mind Nazi money
although he mainly seems to have
wandered into this movie from the set
of the *Maltese Falcon*—so does Peter Lorre,
but at least he gets to read different lines
and learns to fly, but not the way he thought.

After all, this whole story is from the script
of an unproduced Broadway play
which somehow ended up as a movie
where people speak in code—
maybe because they forgot their lines.

Here's looking at you, kid.

About the Author

Michael Minassian is a retired English Professor and spends his time writing, taking photographs, and traveling with his wife both in the U.S. and overseas. He was born in New York City and grew up in New York and New Jersey. In addition to living in Florida, California, North Carolina, Rhode Island, and Texas, he has lived and taught overseas in England, Jamaica, Saudi Arabia, and South Korea. He earned a BA in Political Science at Fairleigh Dickinson University in New Jersey and MA in English with a Certificate in Creative Writing at California State University at Dominguez Hills. For over 30 years he was a member of the English Department at Broward College in South Florida, where he was the Director of an annual Screenwriting Film Festival and also wrote and produced the podcast series "Eye on Literature." In addition, he studied and served as guest tutor for ten years at Cambridge University's Summer Study Program in the UK. He is currently a Contributing Editor for *Verse-Virtual,* an online poetry journal. For more information visit: https://michaelminassian.com

Also by Michael Minassian

A Matter of Timing, 2021 (poetry)
Time is Not a River, 2020 (poetry)
Morning Calm, 2020 (poetry)

Chapbooks:

Jack Pays a Visit, 2022 (poetry)
Chuncheon Journal, 2019 (poetry)
Around The Bend, 2017 (photography)
The Arboriculturist, 2010 (poetry)

Sheila-Na-Gig Editions